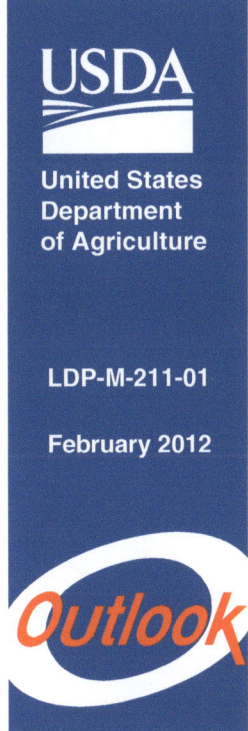

 A Report from the Economic Research Service

www.ers.usda.gov

China's Volatile Pork Industry

Fred Gale, Daniel Marti, and Dinghuan Hu

Contents

Introduction 2
China's Rising Pork Imports
Linked to Domestic Market
Fluctuations. 3
Rising Prices and Costs for
Chinese Pork 6
Cycles in China's Pork
Market 11
Chinese Policies Attempt To
Smooth the Cycle 15
Swine Epidemics Affect the
Pork Market 21
Environmental and Food
Safety Pressures 23
Looking Forward 26
References 27

Approved by USDA's World Agricultural Outlook Board

The use of commercial and trade names does not imply approval or constitute endorsement by USDA.

Abstract

With China's emergence as a new source of potential demand for U.S. pork exports, it is important for U.S. farmers, business leaders, and policymakers to understand the volatile nature of China's pork industry. Prices, hog inventories, and pork output in China fluctuate from year to year in response to various factors that influence the market, and China's imports of pork tend to rise when Chinese hog prices are high. Extensive policy intervention by the Chinese government has contributed to consolidation in the country's pork industry but has not stabilized the market. Imported pork is becoming more competitive in China as Chinese pork production costs rise and animal disease outbreaks, environmental threats, and food safety concerns constrain growth of China's hog industry.

Keywords: Pork, hogs, China, exports, prices, production costs, disease, policy, pollution

Acknowledgments

The authors would like to acknowledge Hongwei Xin of Iowa State University and David Parker, Ariel Szogi, and Brian Kerr of USDA's Agricultural Research Service for providing information about U.S. and Chinese hog manure production and characteristics. The authors would also like to thank Richard Stillman, Mildred Haley, Francis Tuan, John Dyck, Suresh Persaud, and Mary Anne Normile of USDA's Economic Research Service; Dermot Hayes of Iowa State University; Lesley Ahmed, Claire Mezoughem, and Michael Woolsey of USDA's Foreign Agricultural Service; and Ann Seitzinger and Eric Bush of USDA's Animal and Plant Health Inspection Service for helpful comments on the manuscript.

About the Authors

Fred Gale and Daniel Marti are agricultural economists with USDA's Economic Research Service. Dinghuan Hu is a professor with the Institute of Agricultural Economics and Development, Chinese Academy of Agricultural Sciences.

Introduction

China's potential as a major pork importer presents opportunities for hog farmers, business leaders, and investors around the world. Articles and newsletters examining China's effects on the global marketplace reflect buoyant optimism: "The long-run potential for U.S. pork in China is enormous" (Hayes, 2010), and "The potential for further Chinese importation of pork is almost incomprehensible" (a hog industry observer quoted by Dyson (2008)). Announcements of pork sales to China can affect the U.S. market. For example, in October 2009, the *Wall Street Journal* reported "China's pledge to lift a ban on U.S. pork drove prices of lean hogs to a 3-month high on expectations of increased exports to the world's largest pork consumer" (Cui and Waters, 2009).

As China begins to play a larger role in the world pork market, it is important for industry analysts, business leaders, and policymakers to understand the complex factors driving the Chinese hog/pork sector. China's pork industry is constantly buffeted by a range of influences, including disease epidemics, feed prices, policy interventions, seasonal consumption patterns, demand for other meats, and macroeconomic factors. While much attention is focused on the upward trend in commodity prices, pork prices in China tend to rise and fall in multiyear cycles as the industry expands and contracts. The degree of volatility appears to have increased after record-high pork prices in 2007 prompted extensive government intervention and a surge in private investment accelerated structural change in the industry. Following a period of depressed prices in 2010, Chinese pork prices rose to new highs in 2011. China's imports of pork fluctuated in a similar cyclical manner.

This report provides information on volatility in the Chinese pork industry. It reviews recent trends in China-Hong Kong pork imports and fluctuations in Chinese pork prices. It also analyzes the influences of rising feed costs, policy interventions, structural change, and disease epidemics on China's pork industry. As increases in production costs, animal disease epidemics, animal waste disposal challenges, and food safety concerns limit the expansion of China's domestic pork industry, the outlook for pork exports to China is favorable. However, volatility in China's domestic market may result in similar volatility in export sales.

China's Rising Pork Imports Linked to Domestic Market Fluctuations

China's potential to affect the world pork market derives from the size and volatility of its domestic pork market. China accounts for nearly half of the world's pork production and consumption. Its annual pork output is four to five times that of the United States and more than double that of the European Union. According to official Chinese statistics, China slaughters over 600 million hogs annually—one hog for every 2.2 Chinese people.

Historically, China has been a mostly self-sufficient pork economy. Mainland China traditionally imported modest amounts of pork offal and muscle meats and exported a similar amount of pork and live hogs to Hong Kong (a separate customs territory from mainland China). Some pork shipments from other countries to Hong Kong are re-exported to mainland China through "gray" market channels, but the amount is unknown. While Hong Kong is a short distance from the country producing half of the world's pork, most of the territory's imports come from Europe, the United States, and Brazil. From 2000 to 2006, China and Hong Kong combined to import between 500,000 and 600,000 metric tons of pork and pork products annually.[1] These amounts were a significant share of world pork trade but equated to less than 1 percent of annual pork consumption in China-Hong Kong.

China and Hong Kong pork imports surged in 2007 when a shortfall in Chinese pork production led to record Chinese pork prices. That year, Hong Kong-China pork imports nearly doubled to just over 1 million metric tons (mmt), then rose to over 1.9 mmt in 2008 (fig. 1). According to the U.S. Meat

[1] We combine trade statistics for mainland China and Hong Kong since industry sources say that some pork imported to Hong Kong is re-exported to mainland China. Also, Hong Kong's pork imports shift away from mainland China to other suppliers when Chinese prices rise.

Figure 1
China and Hong Kong have become a larger market for pork imports

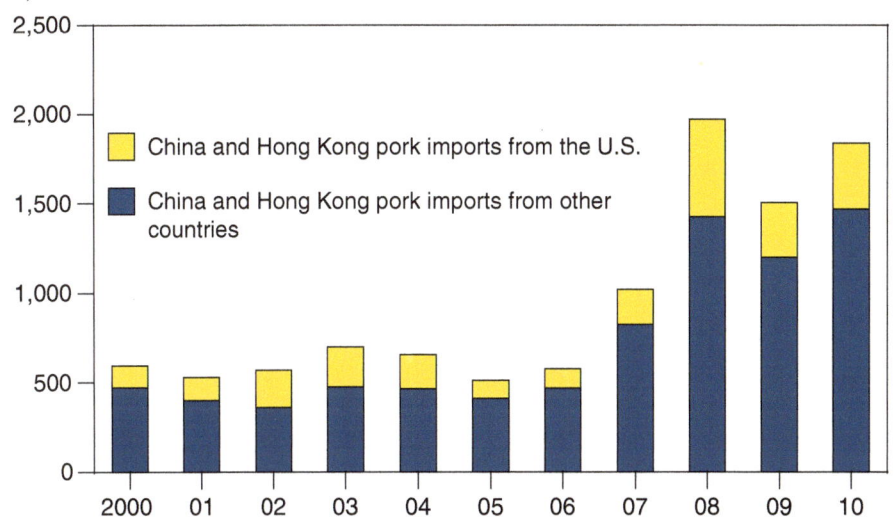

Note: Data include fresh, chilled, and frozen pork; sausage casings; offal; and processed pork products (Harmonized System codes 0203, 020630, 020641, 020649, 0210, 0504, 160241, 160242, 160249).
Source: USDA, Economic Research Service using data from China National Bureau of Statistics and China customs statistics accessed through Global Trade Information Service, Global Trade Atlas.

Export Federation, the 2008 total far surpassed the previous pork-import record of 1 mmt set by Japan in 2005. In 2009, China-Hong Kong pork imports fell to about 1.5 mmt—still nearly three times the pace of imports earlier in the decade—but rebounded to 1.8 mmt in 2010. The 2010 import volume was equivalent to 3.6 percent of China's domestic pork output. The United States supplied about 20 percent of China-Hong Kong pork imports in recent years.

For the U.S. pork industry, China-Hong Kong has been one of the leading export markets since 2007. During the peak import period of 2008, U.S. sales to the region accounted for over 18 percent of U.S. pork exports, about double the annual share exported to China-Hong Kong during 2000-2006.

Monthly statistics on mainland China's pork trade reveal a link between imports and domestic pork prices (fig. 2). High domestic prices during 2007-08 reflected short supplies in the Chinese market and prompted a surge in pork imports. The average domestic hog price in China doubled from about $.52 per pound in the first 4 months of 2007 to a peak of $1.08 per pound in April 2008. Monthly imports by mainland China grew rapidly as prices rose, reaching a peak of 119,000 mt in June 2008, up from 15,000 to 30,000 mt during 2004-06. Imports were boosted by a temporary cut in the country's pork tariff and a state-owned company's contract to purchase U.S. pork to build up reserves ahead of the Olympic Games held in Beijing in August 2008.

After peaking in April 2008, Chinese pork prices fell until early 2009. China's monthly pork imports also fell to under 40,000 mt during the first half of

Figure 2
China monthly pork imports vary with domestic hog price

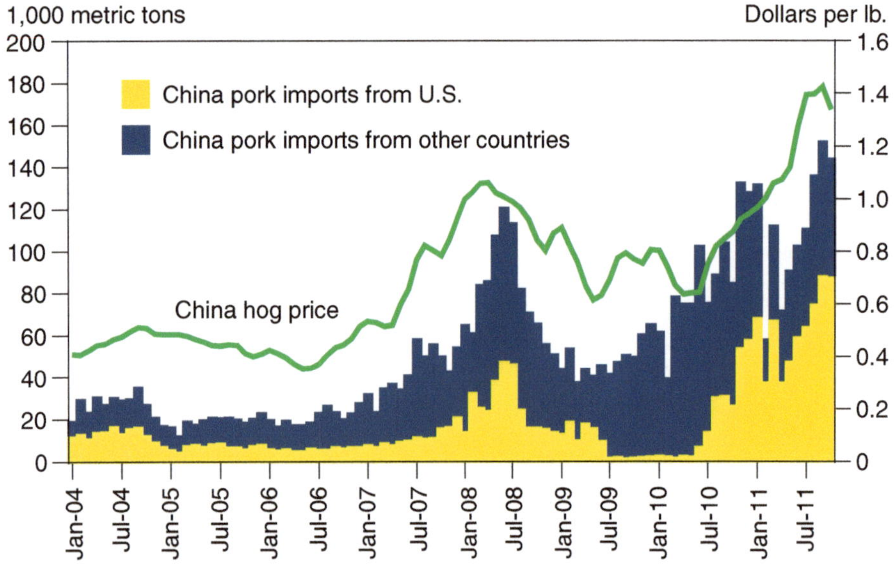

Note: Data include fresh, chilled, and frozen pork; sausage casings; offal; and processed pork products (Harmonized System codes 0203, 020630, 020641, 020649, 0210, 0504, 160241, 160242, 160249). China hog price converted to U.S. dollars at the official exchange rate.
Source: USDA, Economic Research Service using data from China National Bureau of Statistics and China customs statistics accessed through Global Trade Information Service, Global Trade Atlas.

2009. The decline in prices reached a low of $.61 per pound in May 2009, about a year after the peak. A combination of factors helped drive down prices during this period: a buildup in production capacity that increased the domestic supply and a temporary decrease in demand due to concerns among Chinese consumers that the H1N1 influenza virus (swine flu) could be transmitted by eating pork.[2] While no link between pork consumption and H1N1 transmission was scientifically established, Chinese authorities still banned imports of pork from North America to prevent the spread of the disease to China.[3] The ban remained in place for the remainder of 2009 and stopped direct imports of U.S. pork for nearly a year until June 2010.

Chinese pork prices began another run of monthly increases in the second half of 2010 and reached new highs during 2011, 3 years after the sharp increase in prices during 2007-08. With domestic pork prices rising, less expensive foreign pork was more competitive in the Chinese market. Chinese customs statistics revealed that China's monthly pork imports during late 2010 and 2011 surpassed the record pace set in 2008, rising as high as 150,000 mt during September 2011 (see fig. 2). Imports from the United States accounted for most of the import growth during 2011.

[2] According to Zhang (2010), the pork price dropped dramatically during the H1N1 (swine flu) crisis, but consumer confidence recovered rapidly after China's vice minister of agriculture made an announcement to reassure the public that pork was safe to eat.

[3] Chinese authorities also quarantined large numbers of travelers from North America during this period.

Rising Prices and Costs for Chinese Pork

Rising prices in China's domestic pork market were the main contributor to the country's rising pork imports. From 1991 to 2006, Chinese hog prices fluctuated within a relatively narrow range of $.30 per pound to $.50 per pound and were usually less than U.S. prices (fig. 3). After a sharp increase during 2007-08, however, Chinese hog prices have been significantly higher than U.S. hog prices. While Chinese hog prices fell sharply after peaking in 2008, the average price during 2007-10 ($.79 per pound) was more than double the average in 1991-2006 ($.37 per pound). During 2011, prices rose as high as $1.40 per pound.

The shift in prices is an indication of the general improvement of prospects for U.S. pork sales to China. To be cost competitive in China, however, U.S. pork must be comparable in cost or cheaper than Chinese pork after accounting for freight costs, tariffs (12-20 percent), and value-added taxes (13-17 percent). Overall, we estimate that prices in the Chinese market would have to be approximately 30 to 45 percent higher than U.S. prices for U.S. pork to be cost competitive in China.

U.S. and Chinese consumers have complementary tastes that encourage pork trade between the two countries. U.S. consumers prefer muscle meats, while Chinese consumers prefer offal and variety meats that have low value in the United States (Hayes and Clemens, 1997; Fabiosa et al., 2005). As a reflection of these differing preferences, price competitiveness varies for different cuts of pork. In 2011, the average U.S. prices of livers, hearts, hocks, feet, kidneys, and tails were less than half the prices of corresponding parts in a Beijing wholesale market (fig. 4). Prices of all cuts tend to rise and fall to

Figure 3
The average China hog price has risen above the U.S. price

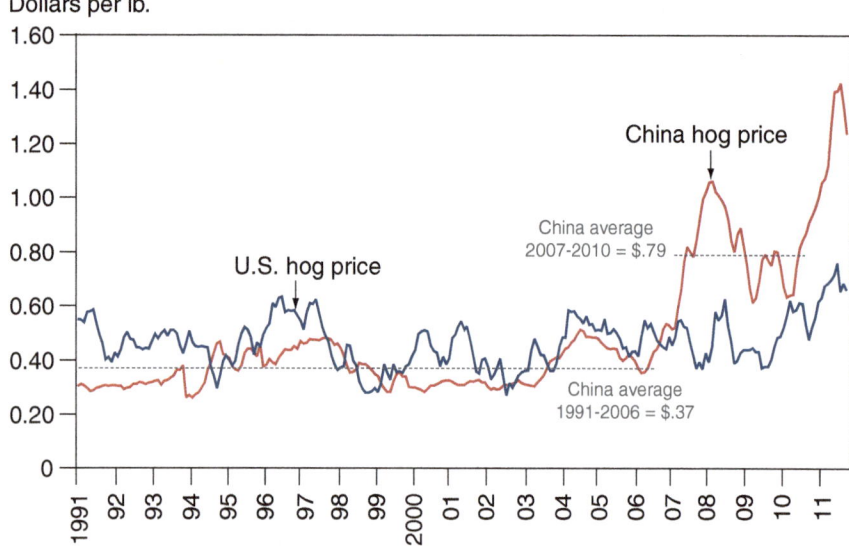

Note: U.S. live hog equivalent, 51-52 percent lean. China price converted to U.S. dollars at official exchange rate. Prices are not adjusted for inflation.

Source: USDA, Economic Research Service using data from USDA, China National Bureau of Statistics, and China Ministry of Agriculture.

Figure 4
Comparison of price of pork parts, U.S. and Beijing averages, 2011

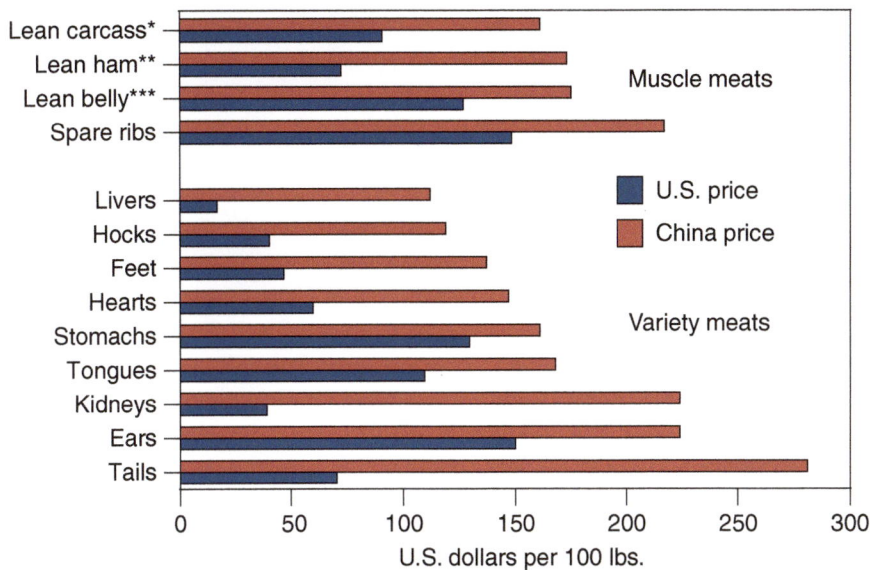

Note: U.S. average price, January-May 2011; China average price from Xinfadi wholesale market, May 2011.
*China lean carcass (bai tiao rou) is compared with U.S. 53-54 percent lean, .65-.80 inches of backfat at last rib.
**China lean ham (hou tun jian) is compared with U.S. composite primal ham.
***China lean belly (wu hua rou) is compared with U.S. composite primal belly.
Source: USDA, Economic Research Service using USDA, Agricultural Marketing Service, LGMN Portal database and Beijing Xinfadi Wholesale Market "price quotations."

reflect general changes in pork prices, and in 2011, the rise in Chinese hog prices drove the prices of both muscle meats and variety meats well above corresponding U.S. prices. For example, the price of a lean carcass in Beijing was about $70 higher than the U.S. carcass price of about $91 per 100 lbs. A year earlier, carcass prices had been nearly equal in the two countries. In mid-2011, muscle meat prices were also relatively high in China. The Beijing price of hams was more than double the U.S. price, the price of spare ribs was nearly 50 percent higher, and the price of bellies was nearly 40 percent higher. Variety meats constitute most of the U.S. pork exported to China, but the widening difference in prices improves the prospects for U.S. muscle meats to be competitive in China.

High pork prices in China likely stem from the rising costs of hog production in China. ERS analysis of data from China's National Development and Reform Commission (NDRC) shows that average hog production costs, converted to U.S. dollars, more than doubled from 2002 to 2009. Chinese hog production costs per pound of live weight rose from about $.30 in 2002 to $.71 in 2010 (fig. 5). Feed is the largest of the hog production expenses in China, accounting for about 60 percent of the total. Feed costs rose from $.18 per pound in 2002 to $.25 per pound in 2006. In 2010, the feed cost rose to $.44 per pound, an increase of 77 percent from 2006. The cost of a feeder pig more than doubled during 2002-10 as well.[4] Estimates of hog production costs for 2011 were not available when this report was prepared, but with corn prices rising, it is likely that feed costs rose further in 2011.

Labor and other expenses may have more of an impact on hog production costs than is indicated in figure 5. China's vibrant labor market and an

[4] Chinese feeder pig prices follow an even more pronounced cyclical pattern than do pork and live hog prices. Feeder pig prices rise during periods of industry expansion and fall when farms are cutting back on production.

Figure 5
China hog production costs are rising

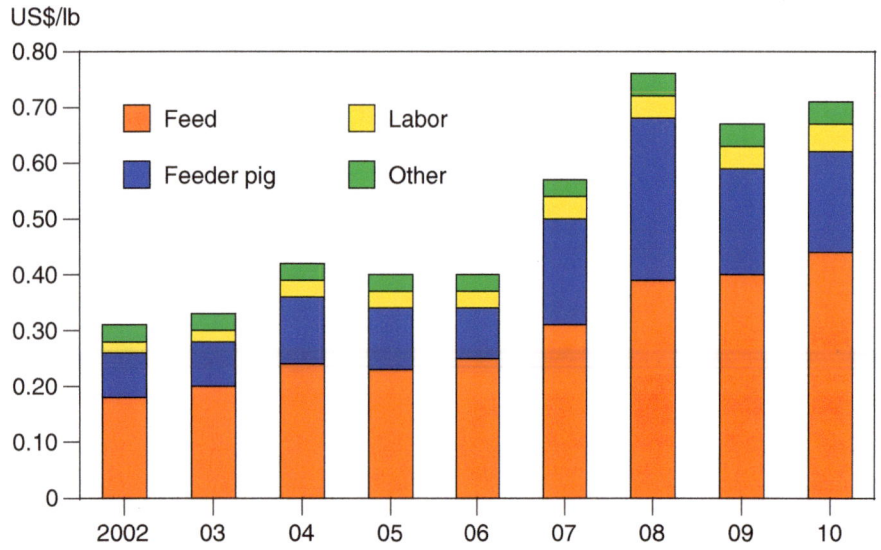

Note: Data in Chinese yuan per head were converted to U.S. dollars per pound of live weight using the official exchange rate. Data are for farms raising 30 or more hogs per year.
Source: USDA, Economic Research Service using data from China National Development and Reform Commission. Data not adjusted for inflation.

increase in school attendance have absorbed slack household labor that was traditionally used for small-scale "backyard" hog production. According to industry reports, the number of rural households raising hogs has been in decline since 2007. And as these small-scale farms exit the industry, they are increasingly being replaced by larger commercial-scale farms operated by companies or farmers who specialize in raising hogs.[5] Compared with small farms, commercial-scale farms have higher overhead costs for housing, equipment, and manure treatment; they purchase higher value breeds of feeder pigs; and they use paid laborers and technicians instead of relying on unpaid family labor. Commercial-scale farms purchase commercial feeds, while small-scale farms use inexpensive crop stalks, bran and hulls from grains, food scraps, and forages.

The increase in feed costs has pushed Chinese hog production costs above those of the United States. Based on data from China and U.S. production cost surveys for 2009, U.S. hog producers had significantly lower costs per pound of live hog weight ($.57) than commercial-scale hog producers in China ($.68) and "backyard" producers in China ($.70) (fig. 6). The U.S. cost advantage was mostly due to lower feed expenses and may be a reflection of a more efficient conversion of feed to meat as well as lower feed prices. Even the Chinese cost advantage in feeder pig prices observed in 2002 by Fabiosa et al. (2005) was reversed after the increase in feeder pig prices during 2007. The Chinese surveys may understate costs of commercial-scale producers by excluding very large 10,000-head farms that are becoming more common in China. These farms have overhead costs that may be comparable to the relatively high "other" costs shown for U.S. farms in figure 6.

Grain prices in China have been rising due to the scarcity of cropland and surging demand for grain by feed mills and industrial users. Chinese hog

[5]Data from the China Ministry of *Agriculture Livestock Industry Yearbook* indicate that approximately half of hogs slaughtered in China in 2010 came from "backyard" farms raising fewer than 50 hogs per year.

Figure 6
U.S. hog production cost advantage due to lower feed cost, 2009

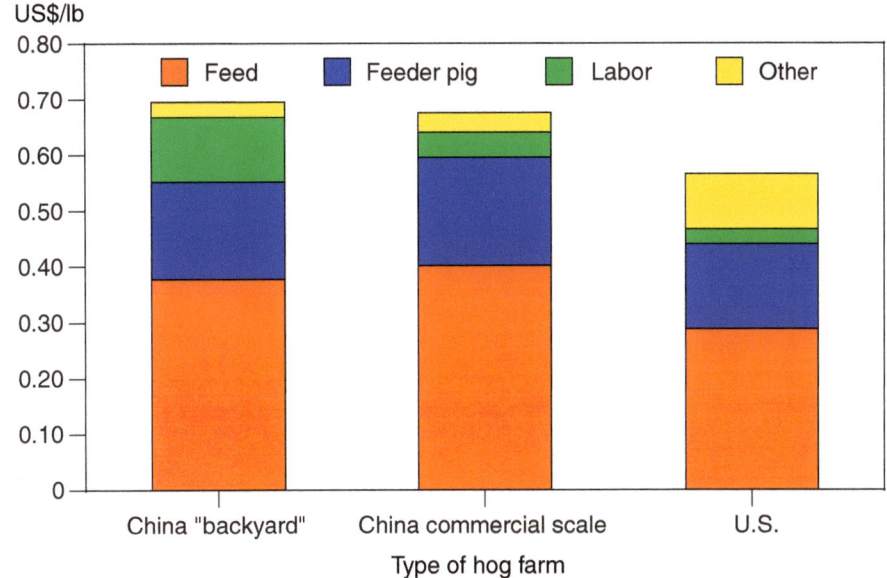

Note: Data in Chinese yuan per head were converted to U.S. dollars per pound of live weight using the official exchange rate. "Backyard" farms raise fewer than 30 hogs per year.
Source: USDA, Economic Research Service using data from China National Development and Reform Commission.

producers and feed mills pay much higher prices for corn than do their U.S. counterparts, and in recent years, rising corn prices have pushed China's feed expenses higher. Rising feed prices tend to push hog and pork prices upward as well.

While the Chinese pork industry still uses a wide variety of feeds, Chinese market analysts focus on the price of corn as an indicator of feed costs (see box, "Wide Variety of Feeds Used"). When high corn prices raise the cost of producing pork in China, industry members may take two approaches to alleviate the cost pressure on Chinese consumers: (1) import corn from the United States or other countries with lower corn prices to reduce the cost of producing pork in China, or (2) import pork produced in countries with lower feed costs. While pork production costs are also rising in the United States, U.S. feed costs remain lower than in China because the United States has more abundant land, water, and grain resources. Meeting Chinese demand for pork by producing hogs near sources of feed in the United States and then exporting pork to China is more cost-efficient than exporting large volumes of grain and oilseeds to produce pork in China (Hayes and Clemens, 1997).

The difference between corn costs in China and those in the United States varies from year to year. Corn prices have generally been rising and are higher in China, but surging U.S. corn prices during 2007-08 and 2010-11 narrowed the gap. A comparison of the monthly average cash prices of corn in Guangdong Province and central Illinois during 2005-10 provides evidence of the cost differential (fig. 7).[6] The Guangdong corn price increased from about $150 per metric ton to over $300 in late 2010. The price of corn in central Illinois was consistently lower than the price in Guangdong, but the difference between the two fluctuated throughout the 5-year period. In early 2010, the Illinois price was less than half the Guangdong price. The large

[6]Guangdong Province is a major hog-producing area in southern China, and it has the largest output of commercial animal feed of any province in China. Corn prices in Guangdong are among the highest in China because little corn is produced there. Several million metric tons of corn are shipped from northeastern China to Guangdong each year.

price difference during mid-2010 stimulated China's first significant corn imports from the United States since the 1990s. (As noted earlier, China's pork imports were also robust during 2010.) U.S. corn sales to China came to a standstill as U.S. corn prices rose and the corn-price difference narrowed later in 2010. However, the Illinois corn price was still 20 percent below the Guangdong price in February 2011.

> **Wide Variety of Feeds Used**
>
> A standard Chinese hog feed ration includes about 60 percent corn and 15 percent soymeal. However, the composition of feed can vary widely across farms. Moreover, feed formulations can vary dramatically by region, by farm size, and over time. Chinese farmers have traditionally fed pigs locally available grains, wheat bran, rice hulls, crop residues, vines, potatoes, food scraps, and byproducts from agricultural processors. The composition of feed depends on the types of materials that are available locally at low cost. Farmers often mix these materials with commercial concentrate feeds that contain soymeal, other protein meals, amino acids, vitamins, and trace elements. An increasing number of farmers use commercial formula feeds that include various combinations of the above items already mixed together. Based on interviews with farmers in Sichuan Province, the proportion of corn in hog feed ranges from 30 to 70 percent, while the proportion of commercial concentrate feeds varies from 10 to 20 percent. Commercial-scale farms account for an increasing share of hog production in China and tend to use a higher proportion of corn and commercial feeds than do smaller farms.

Figure 7
Corn prices are higher in China

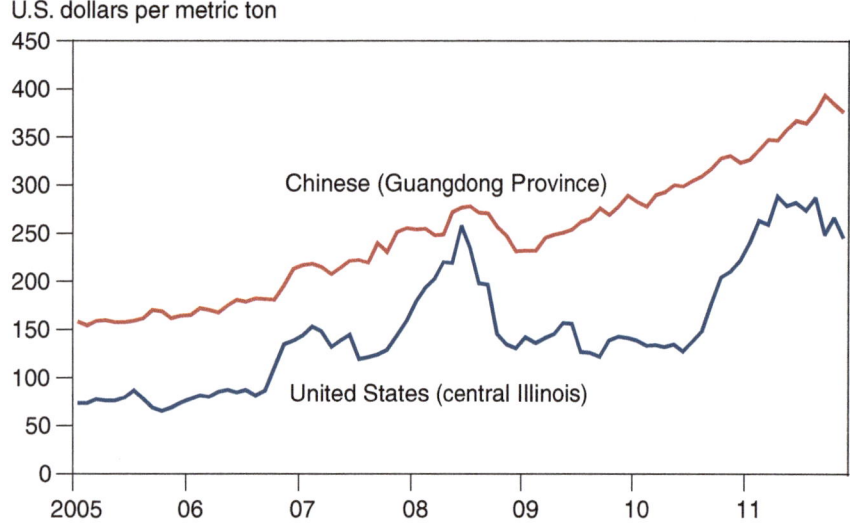

Note: China price converted to U.S. dollars at the official exchange rate.
Source: USDA, Economic Research Service using data from China National Grain and Oils Information Center and USDA.

Cycles in China's Pork Market

The sharp increase in pork prices during 2007 drew attention to the Chinese market's volatility and cycles. Fluctuations in prices and production, however, are not new to the industry. Cyclical patterns in the hog market were recognized in the United States during the 19th century and studied extensively by agricultural economists beginning in the early-20th century (Haas and Ezekiel, 1926). Chinese scholars and analysts have observed similar cyclical fluctuations in China (Liu and Wang 2009; 2010). Zhang (2010a) identified six periods of pork-price increases (1985, 1988, 1994, 1997, 2004, 2007). Several Chinese studies identified a series of four 3- to 4-year cycles in the hog sector during 1996-2009 (Han and Qin, 2007; Liu and Wang, 2009; Nie et al., 2009). The price increase during 2007 prompted Chinese officials to intervene extensively in the pork market to stabilize prices (discussed later in this report).

The well-known "cobweb model" was developed in the 1930s to show how cycles in pork prices can result from the biological lag in supply response (Ezekiel, 1938; Coase and Fowler, 1935). In China, it takes 18-20 months to raise a new generation of gilts to breeding age, produce a crop of pigs, and then raise those pigs to slaughter weight (Zhou, 2010). Thus, when an increase in pork prices prompts farmers to expand production, the corresponding increase in pork supply may take more than a year to enter the market. Conversely, when farmers slaughter sows during a downturn in the market, the sector's ability to expand supply is constrained in future months.

Seasonal fluctuations in demand that correspond to major holidays also affect China's pork market. Hog inventories build up in anticipation of peak demand before the Chinese New Year (usually late January or early February) and the mid-Autumn festival and National Day (mid-September to October 1). In the months following these festival/holiday periods, demand, hog slaughter, and pork prices often decline.

Cycles are evident in the ratio of hog price to corn price, an indicator of short-term profitability in the hog sector. A high ratio indicates that the output price (for hogs) is high relative to the price of the chief input (corn), which typically induces farms to build up hog inventories to increase production. Conversely, a low ratio signals financial losses, which prompt farms to decrease hog inventories.

China's hog-corn price ratio has generally fluctuated around 6:1 (fig. 8, see box, "The Hog-Corn Price Ratio"). A series of fluctuations in China's pork industry are marked by peaks in the ratio early in 2005 and a much higher peak 3 years later in 2008. Periods of low prices and severe losses for hog producers occurred in mid-2006 and mid-2009, again 3 years apart.

The recent cycles resulted from a chain of events that began in 2004 when concerns over an outbreak of avian influenza drove Chinese consumers to substitute pork for poultry meat. The increased demand for pork increased hog prices and encouraged farmers to expand hog inventories. Hog prices peaked in 2005 but subsequently fell as the supply of pork surged. Prices reached a low in mid-2006, and many producers experienced losses and

Figure 8
China hog prices are cyclical

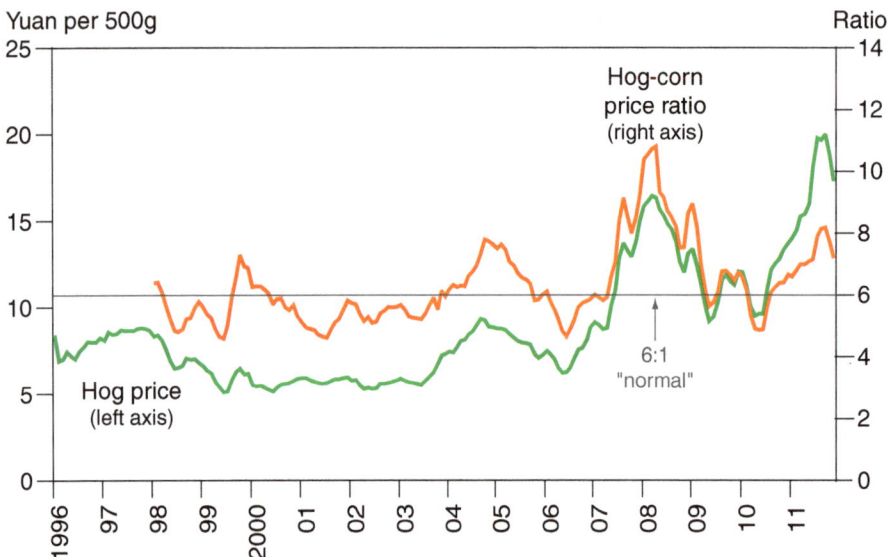

Note: Hog-corn price ratio is a measure of profitability in hog production. Cycles are delineated based on Nie et al., 2009.
Source: USDA, Economic Research Service using data from China National Bureau of Statistics and China Ministry of Agriculture.

culled sows. In late 2006 and 2007, animal disease epidemics reduced the supply of pork, and pork prices again began to rise. The previous year's cull of sows and continuing concerns over the effects of animal diseases constrained the industry's ability to expand production in the short run. Demographic changes also affected the pork supply as off-farm employment and rising incomes encouraged many rural families to purchase pork instead of raising hogs in their backyards. The inelastic shortrun supply contributed to a sharp increase in pork prices.

Rapidly rising pork prices became a national concern in China during 2007. China's consumer price index for meat was up 40 percent year over year, the highest increase among all categories. The jump in pork prices contributed to the country's high inflation rate that year.[7]

An NDRC study of the factors behind rising pork prices during 2007 focused on the tight supply of feeder pigs. The report found that hog prices received by farmers were up 45 percent year-on-year, but that feeder pig prices were up 60 percent. The feeder pig supply was reduced by the culling of sows and the effects of a disease epidemic that caused sows to abort.

High prices for hogs in 2007 and early 2008 attracted investment in large Chinese hog farms and pork processing. Investors included meat, feed, and real estate companies; overseas investment banks; and a well-known Chinese software entrepreneur (Jiao and Kou, 2010). According to official statistics, China's hog inventory grew 5 percent during 2007, and it expanded at a similar pace in 2008. The hog inventory peaked at nearly 470 million head in late 2009, an increase of 51 million from the 2006 total. This marked China's largest expansion of hog inventories since 1996-99.

[7]The increase in China's consumer price index was 12 percent for all food and 4.8 percent for all items during 2007.

The Hog-Corn Price Ratio

The hog-corn price ratio became a valued resource for U.S. commodity market analysts in the 19th century as it reflected the ratio of output price to the price of the main input. At that time, many Midwestern farmers used hogs as an alternative way of marketing corn. When corn prices were low, farmers fed the corn to hogs instead of selling it on the market.

The hog-corn price ratio is now widely used in China as an indicator of hog sector profitability. Market analysts and policymakers in China often view 6:1 as a "normal" level for the ratio. Higher values are considered an indicator of profitability and expansion, while lower values are an indicator of losses and contraction. The breakeven level is often reported to be 5.5:1. The ratio is not as widely used in the U.S. hog industry today because corn accounts for a smaller share of production costs than in years past. The ratio's value as an indicator is also questionable in the Chinese hog industry because corn is only one of many kinds of feeds used by Chinese farmers.

In China, the hog-corn price ratio is computed using prices in yuan per kg. In the United States, the ratio is traditionally computed in dollars per cwt for hogs and dollars per bushel for corn. Because the units used by the two countries differ, the U.S. ratio is typically quoted as a much larger number. Using data from the 1970s, Van Arsdall and Nelson (1984) calculated a breakeven (cash basis) ratio of 15:1 to 16:1, which would be equivalent to 8.5:1 to 9.0:1 calculated using prices in dollars per kg. In a study of historical patterns in the U.S. hog-corn ratio, Holt and Craig (2006) surmised that an increasing trend in the ratio beginning in the 1940s reflected diversification of hog feedstuffs during the post-war period. Recently, U.S. hog market analysts have quoted a higher reference level of 18:1 to 20:1.

Chinese officials regarded the fluctuations in hog prices and profitability beginning in 2007 as evidence of unusual volatility. This prompted extensive government intervention to stabilize the market. However, a comparison with historical U.S. data for 1909-2010 shows that the recent cycles in the Chinese hog-corn price ratio are not unusual (see figure). Chinese fluctuations are similar to cycles that occurred in the United States during the early 20th century. Coase and Fowler's (1935) description of hog cycles in Great Britain during 1920-33 is also remarkably similar to that of recent cycles in China.

Fluctuations in the China hog-corn price ratio are similar to early 20th-century U.S. fluctuations

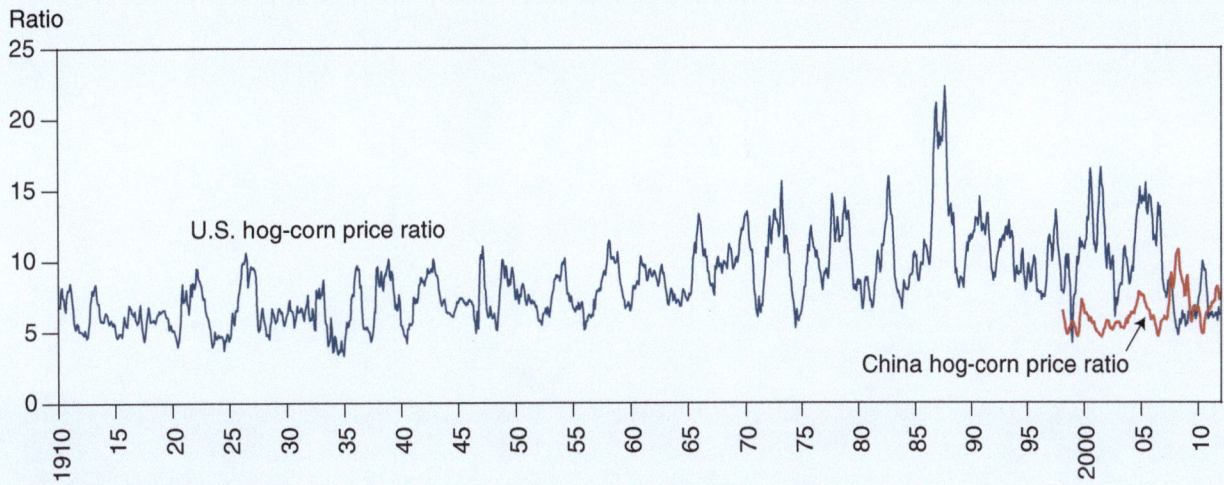

Note: Chart displays monthly ratio of hog to corn price in the United States for 1910-2011 and for China for 1998-2011.

Source: USDA, Economic Research Service analysis of data from USDA, China Ministry of Agriculture and China National Bureau of Statistics.

During 2009 and 2010, two periods of losses and recovery occurred about a year apart, interrupting the pattern of 3-year cycles. The hog-corn price ratio reached a low point in May 2009, about 3 years after the rapid increase in pork prices in 2007. During the second half of 2009, prices rebounded briefly, but the hog-corn price ratio fell again during the first half of 2010 following outbreaks of animal disease epidemics that led to many animal deaths and early slaughter of sick hogs. Furthermore, low prices and economic losses prompted many farmers to cull sows or exit the industry, and China's hog inventory declined during early 2010. Hog prices rebounded in July that year and continued rising during the second half of 2010 and into 2011. The sector returned to profitability during the second half of 2010, but rising corn prices slowed the increase in the hog-corn price ratio. In early 2011, hog prices neared the historical high reached in 2008, and the hog-corn price ratio was 7:1, slightly above "normal." Due to high corn prices, however, the 2011 hog-corn price ratio did not rise as high as it did during the 2008 peak period.

By mid-2011, rising pork prices were again a major influence on China's consumer price index, as they had been in 2007. The sow inventory had yet to recover from the losses and culls of the previous year, and the tight supply of piglets slowed the industry's expansion. High feeder pig prices seemed to be consistent with a limited supply of feeder pigs, and Ministry of Agriculture statistics indicated that sow inventories were down 2-3 percent from a year earlier. In one article, industry analysts expressed unease that the situation would be "a repeat of the 2008 roller coaster" (Sun et al., 2011).

Chinese Policies Attempt To Smooth the Cycle

Chinese officials use a variety of policy measures that are intended to reduce cyclical fluctuations in pork production. Measures include subsidies, tax breaks, and market interventions in hog farming and pork processing. Government officials often play a coordinating role by recruiting farmers as suppliers, arranging access to land and bank loans, and brokering deals with investors or final customers.

In response to the steep increase in pork prices during 2007, the government announced a package of hog-sector subsidies just 2 months after rising pork prices became a subject of public concern (see Zhu, 2007). A series of additional grants, subsidies, and tax breaks aimed at the pork industry followed later in 2007 and in succeeding years. A program introduced in 2009 sought to stabilize pork prices by buying and selling pork for government reserves. The government renewed its emphasis on pork policies in mid-2011 when pork prices surged again.

Pork Industry Subsidies

China's pork policies are part of an ongoing effort to transform the traditional structure of "backyard" farms, small butchers, and pork vendors into a "modern" livestock sector (see box, "Policy Priorities: Modernization and Stability"). Since the 1980s, efforts to modernize the industry have included standardizing hog breeds, feeds, and veterinary medicines; regulating the use of feed additives; enforcing animal health regulations; and shifting toward modern slaughter, processing, and retail markets.

Efforts to modernize China's pork industry were revisited in 2007, a period marked by soaring prices and widespread animal disease epidemics. Officials viewed the prevalence of small-scale backyard farmers as a source of instability because these operations are said to more readily slaughter sows during a market downturn and are more susceptible to animal disease epidemics than larger operations.[8] Officials believe a modernized industry chain will bring stability to the market while also addressing food safety and disease issues.

China's pork policies emphasize improvements in the breeding and farrowing stages of production, upgrading or refurbishing structures and equipment for farms raising slaughter hogs, and attracting investment to the sector.[9] The main policy measures include the following (values converted to U.S. dollars at the official exchange rate in 2010):

- A subsidy payment for each breedable sow set at 50 yuan per head in 2007, raised to 100 yuan ($14.60) in 2008. The sow subsidy was withdrawn in many areas in 2009 but was restored in 2011.

- Subsidized insurance for sows against losses from disease and natural disasters. The premium (paid to a designated insurance company) is 60 yuan ($8.78) per head, of which 12 yuan is paid by farmers and 48 yuan is paid by central and local governments. Initially, the program only

[8] A *Peoples Daily* article blamed the "herd mentality" and "synchronized behavior" of small farmers for market volatility and suggested that intervention cannot stabilize the market as long as small-scale farmers are predominant (Zhang, 2010a). The Ministry of Agriculture asserted that sow subsidies and improved market information prevented a large cull of sows during the period of low prices in 2010 (Sun, 2010).

[9] Only one policy was aimed at pork consumers: small cash subsidies for low-income families and students from poor families to compensate for the rising cost of purchasing pork during a brief period in 2007. Temporary subsidies for general food-price increases were given in late 2010. During 2011, some local governments opened temporary shops selling discounted pork.

covered breedable sows, but it was extended to include gilts in 2011. Pilot programs in some areas insure hogs raised for slaughter.

- Free mandatory immunizations against Porcine Reproductive and Respiratory Syndrome (PRRS, called "blue ear disease" in China), foot-and-mouth disease, and classical swine fever. Vaccines are procured from companies through a bidding process with costs split between central and local government. Vaccines are distributed to farms by veterinary officials.

- A "fine breed" subsidy for artificial insemination using semen from boars of approved breeds (such as Duroc, Landrace, and Yorkshire). The subsidy is 10 yuan ($1.46) for each insemination, for up to 4 attempts per year for each sow.

- Financial awards (grants) of approximately $1 million each to local governments of 362 major pork-supplying counties for financing investments in hog housing, manure handling, immunization, and veterinary work.

- Financial awards to large farms holding at least 500 sows ($146,000) and to standardized farms and village "production zones" where at least 500 hogs are slaughtered annually (from $30,000 to $117,000 according to farm size and province).

- Subsidies of $146,000 were given to each of 300 key breeding farms and provincial hog-breeding centers.

- A waiver of the 25-percent corporate income tax for companies that engage in livestock and poultry production took effect in January 2008 (Petry and Zhang, 2009).

Spending on these programs is only reported on a piecemeal basis by Chinese authorities. The total is difficult to ascertain since there are so many programs, and many are financed jointly by central and local government funds. Central government funds for the "fine breed" subsidy increased from $26 million in 2007 to $95 million in 2010. Pork surplus county awards totaled 3 billion yuan ($450 million) in 2010. Financial awards for large-scale farms totaled $367 million in 2010. Most subsidies are targeted to 362 important pork-producing counties that account for over 40 percent of China's hog production.[10] The award funds are distributed by local authorities to farms, companies, and local officials for refurbishment of hog housing, acquisition of breeding hogs, vaccination programs, manure management, subsidized loans, and support of pork processing, breeding, feed companies and other segments of the industry supply chain.

Various measures are carried out at the local level as experimental pilot programs. These include subsidies for village methane digesters to produce natural gas from hog waste, "ecological" hog-farming projects, subsidized insurance for finishing hogs, funds to pay for disposal of carcasses of diseased hogs, and small cash grants to encourage migrant workers to return to their home villages and set up hog farms.[11] Some of these are extensions of an existing web of local subsidies, model farms, pork reserves, wholesale markets, and supply chain linkages supported by the "vegetable basket responsibility system" in which municipal leaders use various measures to ensure adequate supplies of meat and vegetables for their cities. Pork reserves

[10]These pork counties (*zhu rou chu diao xian*) are important suppliers of pork that produce more pork than they consume. They are chosen by ranking counties using an index based on the number of hogs sold outside the county, volume of hogs slaughtered, and inventory of hogs. The number of counties receiving awards increased each year during 2007-10.

[11]Some of these local programs are financed by the financial awards and other subsidies included in the list above.

Policy Priorities: Modernization and Stability

In 2006, China's vice minister of agriculture gave a speech at a "Modern Livestock Industry Summit" that typifies the government's approach to livestock industry policy. In his remarks, the vice minister stressed the importance of the hog sector's transformation to a modern industry, citing special instructions issued by the country's top leaders. According to the speech, President Hu Jintao had instructed officials to design policy measures to ensure the stable development of the industry, and Premier Wen Jiabao had called for policies that would stabilize hog prices and prevent large fluctuations in pork production.

Promoting a "modern" livestock sector was emphasized in the government's 5-year plan for 2006-10. Modernization includes the related strategies of "industrialization" (*chan ye hua*), "standardization" (*biao zhun hua*), and increased scale of production (*gui mo hua*). These strategies entail concentrating livestock on larger scale farms, making capital investments in farms and processing facilities, disseminating new technologies and equipment, and integrating farms with processors, breeders, and feed mills. The vice minister's speech emphasized the need to nurture strong pork processing companies that would establish well-known brands, play a leadership role in the industry, and improve the industry's competitiveness on the international market. He also encouraged farmers to unite in cooperative organizations. The speech called for livestock industry support measures, including subsidies, tax waivers, earmarked bank loans, and other methods. It also said that the government would experiment with methods for attracting private investment to the pork industry.

The vice minister stated that the livestock industry had experienced unprecedented price fluctuations in recent years, and that the hog industry was recovering from a period of very low prices. He emphasized the importance of improving vaccinations and disease resistance. The speech took place about 6 months before the spread of "blue ear" disease and sharp increases in pork prices in 2007. Many of these policies were implemented during 2008-09, but they failed to prevent an even steeper increase in pork prices during 2010-11.

(both frozen pork and hogs kept in reserve) are held at three levels: central, provincial, and city. In 2011, China's state council ordered large and medium cities in coastal provinces to hold pork reserves to meet 10 days of consumption; other cities were ordered to hold a 7-day reserve.

The implementation of hog sector support varies from year to year and place to place. Local government and bank officials make extra efforts to implement policies when orders are issued from national officials. In 2007, the China Bank Regulatory Commission issued a document ordering banks to make loans to expand pork production capacity. Commercial banks were instructed to lend to companies that raise or slaughter hogs; rural credit cooperatives were instructed to lend to individual hog farmers; and village banks and rural lending companies were instructed to offer production credit. An account by journalists described how local officials in a county of Sichuan Province organized a meeting in 2007 to urge farmers to raise hogs and offer them subsidies while bank officials went door to door to offer loans secured by personal property like ceiling fans and washing machines.

In coastal provinces, hog production is increasingly dominated by large-scale farms operated by companies. In some cities, hog production is banned due to environmental concerns. In western provinces, slaughter hogs are usually raised by individual small-scale farmers, but officials encourage companies to invest in large breeding and farrowing farms that supply feeder pigs. In 2007 and subsequent years, Ministry of Agriculture officials accelerated implementation of a plan to subsidize construction of "livestock production zones" (*yang zhi xiao qu*) where individual farmers may concentrate their animals in facilities that simulate large-scale farms. In 2011, China's State Council announced a plan to allocate 2.5 billion yuan ($385 million) annually over 5 years for construction of large-scale hog farms.

In 2007, the combination of policies and high prices attracted investment in new farms, slaughter and processing plants, and imported breeding animals. The buildup of production capacity stimulated by policies helped drive prices down during 2008-09 nearly as fast as they had risen during 2007. Meat sector analysts attributed falling prices to excess supply of pork, with some citing the influx of investment due to government policies as a chief cause (Yi Zhang, 2010, Feng, 2004; Xiao and Wang, 2009).

"Price Alert" Market Stabilization

In 2009, Chinese policymakers introduced a "hog price alert" market intervention program aimed at reducing the cyclical variation in hog prices. The program's main function is to buy up pork for reserves to increase demand when prices are low and sell pork to augment supply when prices are high. The program intends to stabilize hog inventories by preventing extended periods of low prices that might prompt large culls of sows.[12]

According to documents describing the program, movements in the hog-corn price ratio and several other designated market indicators trigger purchases and sales of pork reserves. The program specifies the "normal" range for the ratio as 6:1 to 9:1, and authorities may take measures to prevent the hog-corn price ratio from falling below 5.5:1.[13] When the ratio falls in various ranges below 6:1, authorities can order designated meat companies to purchase frozen pork to hold in reserve (table 1)[14] When the ratio is 5.5:1 to 6:1, provincial documents specify that cities should maintain a 7-day reserve of pork (based on average consumption of 100 grams/person/day).[15] When the ratio falls below 5.5:1, the central government can subsidize interest on loans to slaughter and processing companies to encourage them to increase inventories of pork and increase output of processed pork products. Also, the government can authorize an increase in central meat reserves and local reserves in large cities. At "abnormally low" levels below 5:1, the program calls for large increases in reserves, and officials can authorize one-time subsidies per sow for farmers in major pork-producing counties to prevent slaughter of sows. The document also calls for limits on pork imports "to reduce market supply" and increases in pork exports by raising food safety standards and providing technical, information, and policy support.[16] When the hog-grain price ratio exceeds 9:1, the government can sell frozen pork reserves to bring down prices, and it may issue subsidies to low-income consumers.

Since the program's inception, China's NDRC has published weekly average prices and monthly hog inventory and slaughter on a web site (www.gov.cn/zfjg/szsctk.htm). However, little information about purchases and sales of pork under the program is revealed. News media reports reveal that purchases and sales have taken place, but details on amounts or locations of the transactions are seldom announced.

[12]A large cull of sows constrains the sector's ability to expand production in later months. This phenomenon was blamed for the sharp increase in pork prices in 2007.

[13]Provincial guidelines specify that the ratio is to be calculated using the provincial average live hog price received by farmers and the wholesale price of corn. Secondary targets stated in the National Development and Reform Commission document are to prevent the ratio of feeder pig-to-hog carcass (*bai tiao rou*) prices from falling below 0.7:1, maintain hog inventories of at least 410 million head, and maintain sow inventories of at least 41 million head.

[14]Provincial documents for implementing the program set 6:1 as the breakeven point for the hog-corn price ratio, but officials may adjust the targets based on changes in industry structure and other factors. Henan Province's document set the breakeven point at 7:1, and Zhejiang Province set it at 6.5:1.

[15]Zhejiang Province specified a 7-day supply of reserve pork for its three largest cities and a 3-day supply for other cities. As noted on page 19, the national required reserve for large cities was raised to a 10-day supply in 2011.

[16]The means of limiting imports are not specified. The Shandong Province document explains that the provincial branch of the inspection and quarantine bureau will work with other departments to implement temporary policies to limit imports.

Table 1
China's pork market intervention guidelines

Hog-grain price ratio[1]	Color code	Government action
Over 9:1		Sell frozen pork reserves into the market; issue subsidies to low-income consumers.
6:1 to 9:1	Green ("normal")	Monitor markets and price fluctuations; issue information. Pork reserves mainly used for emergencies and disasters.
5.5:1 to 6:1	Blue	Add to central and local pork reserves when ratio is in this range for 4 consecutive weeks.
5:1 to 5.5:1	Yellow	Subsidize interest on loans to large meat processing companies to encourage them to add to commercial reserves and increase pork processing.
Under 5:1	Red	Increase central reserves and require large and medium cities to increase local reserves of frozen pork when the ratio is in this range for 4 consecutive weeks. The number of live hogs kept in reserve may be increased. If the ratio is still in this range after reserve purchases, a temporary subsidy of 100 yuan per sow may be given to farms in main hog-producing counties when sow inventory is down 5 percent year-on-year. Appropriately limit pork imports to reduce the market supply; "improve" the food safety system to encourage pork exports.

[1]Some provinces set a higher threshold for the hog-grain price ratio.

Source: USDA, Economic Research Service using National Development and Reform Commission, *Regulatory plan for controlling excessive hog price declines*, Bulletin No. 1, January 9, 2009, and provincial guidelines for implementation.

The first intervention under the stabilization program occurred in May 2009, less than 6 months after its introduction (fig. 9). The hog-grain price ratio fell below 6:1, and the government began purchasing pork for reserves in mid-June 2009. During April-June 2010, the government conducted five rounds of pork purchases before prices rebounded in July. Official reports said the hog-grain price ratio fell from 5.07 in mid-April to 4.81 by May 26, well into the "red" region specified by the program. It was still in the red region when the fifth round of purchases was carried out at the end of June 2010. NDRC reported that the hog-grain price ratio reached the 6:1 normal level in late July.

Later in 2010, the government ordered sales of pork reserves when pork prices began to rise rapidly. Hog prices rose more than 20 percent during July-November 2010. A round of frozen pork sales was ordered to prevent excessive price increases ahead of the October 1 National Day holiday, and a second round was ordered in November. Some local authorities sold pork reserves in mid-2011 as pork prices reached record levels. These sales occurred when the hog-corn price was far below the 9:1 ratio specified for triggering such sales.

During 2011, as pork prices again became a national concern, there were scattered reports of pork reserve sales by some local authorities but no coordinated national campaign to sell pork reserves. Instead, the State Council issued a new directive ordering local authorities to increase their pork reserves. Large and medium cities and cities in coastal areas were directed to maintain a reserve equivalent to 10 days of pork consumption, and other cities were directed to maintain a 7-day reserve.

The influence of the price alert program on pork prices is hard to discern, especially since the amount, timing, and location of pork reserve purchases and sales are not announced. The program's ability to affect the market is

Figure 9
China's sow inventory follows changes in hog-corn price ratio

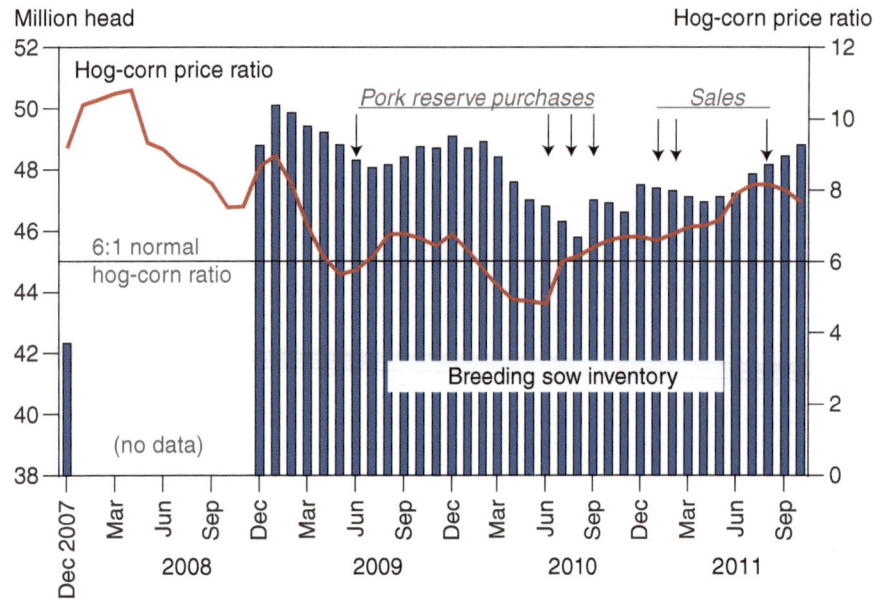

Source: USDA, Economic Research Service using data from China Ministry of Agriculture.

limited because frozen pork purchases constitute a tiny portion of a huge, scattered market. Zhang and Nie (2010) reported that reserve purchases in 2009 totaled 110,000 metric tons, equivalent to just 0.26 percent of China's annual pork output. The Agricultural Development Bank of China reported that it financed meat-reserve purchases of 250,000 metric tons in 2010, about 0.5 percent of annual pork production.[17] Frozen pork itself constitutes a relatively small part of the market because Chinese consumers have a strong preference for freshly slaughtered meat.[18]

Officials credited the first round of purchases in 2009 for bringing about a recovery of pork prices that year, but this seems unlikely since authorities were still recruiting companies to hold reserves and many provinces had not even released their implementation regulations at that time. Some market reports again credited reserve purchases for the rebound in hog prices in July 2010, but the rebound was more likely due to a 5.7-percent decrease in hog slaughter that month.

The weakness of the hog price alert program was revealed by the sharp increase in pork prices during 2010-11. During this period, rising food prices were a major policy concern in China and officials ordered sales of pork in the fall of 2010, yet hog prices rose 40-to-50 percent and by June 2011 pork prices reached the record level set in early 2008. Market reports ascribed the surge in prices to short supplies of pork, which resulted from widespread animal disease, culls of sows, and exits from the industry during the period of low prices and losses in 2010. The supply of feeder pigs in 2011 was limited by the cull of sows a year earlier, while rapid income growth created robust demand (Woolsey and Zhang, 2011). The wide swing in prices and hog inventories during 2010-11 was remarkably similar to that of 2006-07—exactly the type of phenomenon that the price alert policy was intended to prevent.

[17]This total may include modest amounts of other meats in addition to pork.

[18]Liu and Sun (2010) estimated that all sales of chilled, frozen, and processed pork together account for less than 10 percent of China's pork market.

Swine Epidemics Affect the Pork Market

Outbreaks of "blue ear" disease (PRRS), foot-and-mouth disease (FMD), classical swine fever, pneumonia, streptococcus suis, circovirus, parasites, and erysipelas (a bacterial infection of the skin) are common in China's hog industry. News reports indicate that large losses attributed to disease periodically restrict the supply of pork, contributing to price surges. Chinese news media periodically report illegal sale of pork from diseased hogs, pork that is discolored or bearing lesions, and discovery of large numbers of hog carcasses in rivers and canals.

The impact of disease on the pork market is impossible to assess with any precision. When disease affects sows and young pigs, impacts on the market may occur several months after an outbreak. The frequency and incidence of disease is hard to measure accurately, and outbreaks are often regional. While the Ministry of Agriculture reports on disease outbreaks, these figures likely understate the actual incidence of disease because farmers and merchants have little incentive to report diseased animals to authorities (Woolsey et al., 2010).

Rising pork prices in 2007 and 2011 were attributed in part to disease outbreaks. During 2006-07, the supply of feeder pigs was reduced in part because blue ear disease caused sows to abort. This restricted the supply of finished hogs and led to high prices during 2007-08. During 2010, another round of disease outbreaks induced many farmers to slaughter hogs early, and many diseased carcasses were illegally sold to slaughterhouses. The increased supply of slaughtered hogs and the prevalence of tainted pork led to a period of depressed prices during 2010 (see Woolsey et al., 2010). The disease-related decline in hog inventories during 2010 led to tight supplies of feeder pigs and another surge in pork prices during 2011 (Woolsey and Zhang, 2011; Sun et al., 2011).

Chinese agricultural officials have taken steps to reduce the effects of animal disease epidemics. Immunizations for PRRS, classical swine fever, and FMD disease are compulsory and subsidized. Farmers are compensated for culling animals to prevent epidemics, and local officials must bear the cost of sanitary disposal of dead animals. Agricultural officials have made it a priority to improve veterinary services, biosafety, and monitoring and control of farms, slaughterhouses, transportation, and markets. Chinese pigs are required to have ear tags recording 7 to 8 mandatory immunizations. Slaughterhouses are required to ensure that hogs have ear tags and vaccination certificates. Inspectors are required to conduct ante- and post-mortem inspections of slaughtered hogs, and tissue samples are to be examined for parasites at slaughterhouses.

However, government programs and regulations are not uniformly implemented, and problems with animal health persist. Vaccines may not be effective against multiple strains of PRRS that exist in China's hog herds. Wang (2009) reported that ear tags (that record immunizations) and animal quarantine certificates can be easily falsified or purchased; farmers often miss vaccinations; syringes are often used on multiple animals; and veterinary personnel needed to carry out vaccinations are in short supply. In a small survey of farmers, Liu et al. (2007) found most farmers whose sick pigs did not respond to treatment sold the animals before they died or improperly discarded the carcasses of dead animals (only one farmer said he buried dead pigs as required by regulations). Liu et al. found that most farmers did not use ear tags or only attached them at the time the pigs were sold; pigs without ear tags were sold to unlicensed butchers or neighboring farmers.

The high density of animal populations, rudimentary facilities, lack of technical knowledge among farm personnel, and lack of resistance among "foreign" breeds of pigs may contribute to vulnerability to disease. One article in a Chinese veterinary publication warned farmers that changes in feed, poor nutrition, neglect of immunizations, and other animal stress-inducing factors that are more common on small-scale farms may heighten risk of classical swine fever outbreaks (Ren, 2010). According to Feng (2010), periods of extreme weather or flooding can trigger an epidemic among farms characterized by stressed animals and neglect of immunizations.[19] As evidence of farmers' cost-cutting, Feng noted that many feed and veterinary drug companies reported sales declines of as much as 30 percent during the period of losses in 2010. Feng also suggested that periods of losses by farmers may leave local governments short of cash to pay veterinary technicians and dispose of carcasses.

Feng (2010) hypothesized that disease outbreaks may actually be linked to the hog cycle itself. Writing in an industry newsletter, he observed that extended periods of losses for small- and medium-scale hog farmers may leave them short of cash. Farmers may then cut costs by switching to lower quality, less-nutritious feeds, and neglect vaccinations. Less nutritious diets leave animals in a weakened state and vulnerable to disease. Jiao and Kou (2010) reported that farmers in Sichuan cut costs during a period of depressed prices by increasing the proportion of rapeseed stalks in hog rations. Sun et al. (2011) observed that the substitution of cheaper feed substitutes contributed to chronic disease problems in the industry.

Chinese officials introduced subsidized insurance for producers of sows to reduce the risk of financial losses attributed to animal deaths, but some market reports indicate that this program encountered moral hazard problems. Liu (2010) reported heavy losses incurred by companies offering sow insurance in Henan Province, citing large numbers of claims, high costs, and fraud.[20] In July 2010, a Yangzhou newspaper reported that the insurance company's payouts for sow death losses had doubled from the previous year and reached 25 percent in one county (Yang, 2010). According to an insurance worker quoted in the article, some farmers neglected to treat sows for diseases during periods of low hog prices because the insurance indemnity exceeded the animal's salvage value if it were culled and sold.

---

[19]Woolsey et al. (2010) also report that low efficacy of free vaccines may contribute to epidemics. Some local distributors lack facilities to keep vaccines at the proper temperature.

[20]A company official told Liu that in some cases, multiple farmers filed claims on the same dead animal.

Environmental and Food Safety Pressures

Producing large quantities of pork in China entails "external" costs—the environmental impacts of hog waste and risks of food safety incidents—that are not factored into the market price of pork. According to Wang et al. (2006), one Chinese hog produces 5.3 kg of waste daily, which contains large amounts of nutrients not absorbed by the animal as well as heavy metals and pharmaceutical residues. During the 1950s and 1960s, Chinese officials encouraged individual households to raise hogs as a means of producing organic fertilizer to spread on fields to raise grain yields. In later decades, chemical fertilizer became available and the rising demand for meat prompted a large increase in the number of hogs. Consequently, the production of manure exceeded the capacity of the surrounding farmland to absorb its nutrients. Small farms rarely treat manure, but large farms are usually required to invest in treatment facilities. Gao et al. (2006) estimated that 80 percent of commercial-scale farms lack equipment and facilities to properly dispose of waste, which causes "serious pollution of water, soil, and air and threatens the health of animals and humans." Waste often washes into streams and rivers, fouling drinking water and contributing to eutrophication (nutrient enrichment) of major bodies of water.

Several Chinese studies estimated that pollution from livestock farms totaled roughly 3 billion metric tons annually, about three times the pollution emitted from industrial sources (Gao et al., 2006; Liu, 2009; and Wang et al., 2006). Gao et al. estimated China's hog waste at 1.29 billion metric tons annually, 47 percent of the total livestock and poultry waste generated. A census of pollution sources released in 2009 found that livestock waste was a chief cause of water pollution in China (China Ministry of Environmental Protection, 2010).

While Chinese officials are taking steps to address these problems, the dense population of hogs strains the capacity of the land to supply feed for hogs and absorb their waste and also makes it difficult to control and prevent animal diseases (FAO, 2006). China has many regions with high hog population densities. ERS calculations using provincial- and state-level data on hog inventories and cropland for China and the United States show that China had 94 hogs for every 100 acres of cropland nationwide at year end in 2008, more than 4 times the U.S. ratio of 20 hogs per 100 acres (table 2). In many of China's leading hog-producing provinces, the density exceeded 100 hogs per 100 acres, and the density exceeded 200 in Sichuan, Hunan, and Guangdong Provinces. North Carolina was the only U.S. State with over 200 hogs per 100 acres (similar to the density in Sichuan), and Iowa had 82 (slightly below the China average and similar to the density in Hebei and Jiangsu Provinces). Other U.S. States had densities of fewer than 40 hogs per 100 acres, far less than in China. With an already-high density of hogs, the environmental impact of hog production and tight supplies of feed may constrain growth of China's hog industry.

Table 2
Comparison of hog population density in China and United States, 2008

	Hog population	Hog-cropland density		Hog population	Hog-cropland density
	Million head	*Hogs per 100 acres*		*Million head*	*Hogs per 100 acres*
China	462.9	94		66.7	20
Leading provinces:			Leading States:		
Sichuan	53.3	221	Iowa	19.8	82
Henan	44.6	139	North Carolina	9.6	225
Hunan	39.2	255	Minnesota	7.4	37
Shandong	27.3	90	Illinois	4.4	19
Yunnan	26.7	109	Indiana	3.5	29
Hubei	24.6	130	Nebraska	3.4	17
Guangdong	23.8	206	Missouri	3.1	23
Guangxi	23.1	135	Oklahoma	2.4	26
Hebei	20.2	79	Ohio	1.9	19
Jiangsu	17.2	89	Kansas	1.7	7

Note: Hog population is year-end inventory. Density is the ratio of hog inventory to total cropland. Provinces and States are ranked by hog population; only the top 10 are shown.

Source: USDA, Economic Research Service using data from China National Bureau of Statistics and USDA, National Agricultural Statistics Service.

Chinese officials are promoting "ecological" modes of hog production that use hog waste to feed fish or fertilize crops and use bacteria to break down hog waste. China's 2011-2015 5-year plan will emphasize the importance of controlling livestock waste (Zhang, 2010b). However, a number of cities and provinces in China have introduced regulations that ban hog farms and slaughterhouses from operating near residential areas and waterways. Draft regulations prepared by Shandong Province in 2010 banned new livestock farms in urban areas, near sources of drinking water, in scenic areas, and in places where toxic substances exceed prescribed limits.

Food safety is also a major concern for Chinese consumers of pork. The news media in China has frequently reported on the hog industry's use of clenbuterol and other illegal feed additives, the slaughter of sick hogs, the pumping of potentially contaminated water into hogs prior to slaughter, and the contamination of feed with heavy metals. Chinese consumers are also becoming more wary of pork products that contain dyes, preservatives, and other food additives. In March 2011, a widely publicized report that a subsidiary of China's largest processed pork manufacturer purchased hogs raised with illegal feed additives had little direct impact on the pork market (Woolsey and Zhang, 2011). However, industry reports claim that the incident helped drive the trend toward consolidation of hog farms discussed earlier in this report. For example, the company implicated in the incident pledged to open a 10,000-head company-operated farm to supply each slaughterhouse it builds to gain more control over the production process.

Food safety concerns are also contributing to changes in purchase patterns that may make consumers more receptive to imported pork. Traditionally, Chinese consumers preferred to purchase freshly slaughtered pork from small wet market vendors, but food safety concerns have encouraged them to shift purchases to supermarkets where pork is believed to be more sanitary and free of illegal feed additives. Government plans to consolidate slaughterhouses by 2015 entail an increase in interregional trade in chilled or frozen pork. The diminishing role of localized wet markets and the development of modern market channels with cold chain facilities may create more opportunities for imported pork to reach Chinese consumers. Many Chinese consumers responded to the dairy industry's melamine adulteration crisis by purchasing imported milk products, and demand for imported pork could similarly be boosted by domestic food safety concerns.

Looking Forward

China's status as a major pork importer will likely continue to grow. China's tradition of self-sufficiency in pork will be hard to maintain as feed costs rise and as land for expanding farms and processing facilities becomes scarce and expensive. The environmental and food safety impacts of producing large numbers of hogs in China will become more apparent. Interregional shipments of pork within China are limited by lack of reliable transportation and temperature-controlled storage.

Stricter regulatory enforcement in the United States, greater investments in animal housing and manure handling, wider dissemination of technical expertise, and closer coordination between producers and processing companies help U.S. farmers produce pork with less of an impact on the environment, fewer food safety incidents, and fewer disease outbreaks than in China. Demand from China raises the value of variety meats and offal that are not widely used as food in the U.S. market.

Chinese restaurant chains, hotels, and other buyers who demand pork with high and consistent quality are important potential customers for imported pork (Fabiosa et al., 2005). With diversifying consumer tastes and growing segmentation in the market, imported pork can coexist in the Chinese market with domestic grain-fed pork and meat from local pig breeds.[21]

Strong resistance to pork imports in China can disrupt trade and affect exporters. China lowered tariffs on pork after its accession to the World Trade Organization, but pork imports still face resistance similar to that described by Hayes and Clemens (1997). Evidence of this can be seen among the policy responses listed in the Chinese "hog price alert" program, which include unspecified "limits" on imported pork to reduce the market supply and "encouragement" of pork exports. When Chinese pork prices were soaring in 2007, officials made announcements to assure the public that China would not import large amounts of pork (Xinhua, 2007).[22] In June 2010 (after China lifted its H1N1-related ban on U.S. pork), an article entitled "Be on Guard! American Pork's 'Soybean Appetite'" warned that imports could "eat up" China's pork industry if the industry was not protected (Li, 2009). An analyst quoted in the article cautioned readers to "Be careful of the trap set by the Americans," warning that if U.S. pork imports are not limited, the pork industry "…is likely to repeat the mistakes of the soybean industry with disastrous consequences."[23] Similarly, Liu (2010) reported that Chinese officials were wary of foreign investment in the pork industry because officials feared losing "guidance power" over the industry.

---

[21] Many supermarkets and specialty retail shops in China offer pork from local pig breeds. The appeal of this pork, generally sold at premium prices, is its stronger flavor and purported health benefits.

[22] Articles from official media included assurances that imported pork was purchased mainly by hotels, that imports would not affect the market, and that China has free trade in pork but also a strict inspection and quarantine system.

[23] This refers to China's high reliance on soybean imports.

References

China Animal Husbandry Information Center. "Jiedu Di Wu Ci Shouchu 'Zai Du Chu Shou' Ken Hou Yuanyi (Interpreting Reasons Behind the Fifth Purchase of Reserves)." July 2, 2010. http://livestock.feedtrade.com.cn/

China Ministry of Agriculture. *Livestock Industry Yearbook*. Beijing: China Agriculture Press, various years.

China Ministry of Environmental Protection, National Bureau of Statistics, and Ministry of Agriculture. *Di Yi Ci Quan Guo Wuran Yuan Pucha Gongbao* (Communique of the First National Census of Pollution Sources). Posted by Xinhua News Service, February 9, 2010. http://news.xinhuanet.com/politics/2010-02/09/content_12960555.htm

China Ministry of Finance. *Ministry of Finance Notice on Rising Pork Prices and Promotion of Healthy Development of the Hog Industry* (in Chinese). No. (2007)221, June 18, 2007.

China National Development and Reform Commission (NDRC)/Ministry of Agriculture. *Declaration of Hog Standardization, Large Scale Farms (Zones), Hog and Poultry Breeding Construction Project Plan* (in Chinese). NDRC Rural Economy No.(2008)524, March 3, 2008.

China National Development and Reform Commission (NDRC), Office of Price. "2007 Nian Shang Ban Nian Shengzhu Chengben, Shouyi, Jiage Jun Chuang Lishi Xin Gao (Hog Production Cost, Profit and Price for the First Half of 2007—Price Reaches a New Historical High)." September 5, 2007. http://jgs.ndrc.gov.cn/jgqk/t20070905_157541.htm

Coase, R.H., and R.F. Fowler. "Bacon Production and the Pig-cycle in Great Britain," *Economica*, May 1935, pp. 142-167.

Cui, Carolyn, and Theopolis Waters. "Hog Prices Hit 3-Month High as China Vows to End Pork Ban," *Wall Street Journal*, October 30, 2009. http://online.wsj.com/article/SB125682230437515867.html

Dyson, Tom. "How We'll Make a Fortune Exporting Pork to China," *Daily Wealth*, July 30, 2008. www.dailywealth.com

Ezekiel, M. "The Cobweb Theorem," *Quarterly Journal of Economics*, Vol. 53, 1938, pp. 255-80.

FAO (Food and Agriculture Organization of the United Nations). *Livestock's Long Shadow: Environmental Issues and Actions*. Rome: FAO, 2006.

Fabiosa, J., Dinghuan Hu, and Cheng Fang. *A Case Study of China's Commercial Pork Value Chain*. MATRIC Research Paper 05-MRP 11, Iowa State University, August 2005. http://www.card.iastate.edu/publications/synopsis.aspx?id=788

Feng, Yuhui. "The Hog Market Welcomes Its Longest Profit Cycle in 10 Years" (in Chinese). China Feed Industry Association, unpublished market analysis, 2004. http://www.xqyzz.cn/file/sc05.htm

_____. "An investigation of hog and sow inventory changes in several regions" (in Chinese), *China Journal of Animal Science*, June 2006.

_____. *Soozhu China Pork Market Analysis and Warning Report* (in Chinese). Zhong Ke Yi Heng Modern Agriculture Information Institute (Beijing) weekly newsletter, June 2010.

Gao, Ding, Tongbin Chen, Bin Liu, Yuanming Chen, Guodi Zheng, and Yanxia Li. "Releases of Pollutants From Poultry Manure in China and Recommended Strategies for the Pollution Prevention" (in Chinese), *Geographical Research*, 2006, Vol. 25, No. 2, pp. 311-319.

Haas, G.C., and M. Ezekiel. *Factors Affecting the Price of Hogs*. U.S. Department of Agriculture Bulletin 1440, 1926.

Han, Jie. "Finance Ministry Allocated 6.5 Billion Yuan in Funds for Sow Insurance and Subsidy" (in Chinese). Xinhua News Agency, June 26, 2007.

Han, Jun, and Zhongchun Qin. "Analysis of Our Country's New Round of Hog Cycle Fluctuations" (in Chinese). Special manuscript, State Council Development Research Center, August 2007, and *Today's Animal Husbandry and Veterinary Review*, September 2007.

Hayes, D.J. "The Potential Market for U.S. Pork Exports in China," Iowa State University Working Paper, January 13, 2010.

Hayes, D.J., and Roxanne Clemens, "The Chinese Market for U.S. Pork Exports," Iowa State University CARD Briefing Paper 97-BP 14, March 1997.

Holt, M.T., and L.A. Craig. "Nonlinear Dynamics and Structural Change in the U.S. Hog-Corn Cycle: A Time-Varying STAR Approach," *American Journal of Agricultural Economics*, Vol. 88, No. 1 (February 2006), pp. 215-233.

Jiao, Jian, and Bo Kou. "Wen Luan 'Zhu Zhouqi' (Disorderly 'Hog Cycle')" (in Chinese), *Caijing Magazine*, No. 13, 2010.

Li, Jinling. "*Jingti! Meiguo Zhuroude 'Dadou Weikou'*" (Be on Guard! American Pork's 'Soybean Appetite.') *Zhongguo Chanjing Xinwen* (China Industry and Economic News), May 26, 2009. http://finance.sina.com.cn/roll/20100526/18538007356.shtml

Liu, Fang. "*Zhengce Zhu PK Shichang Zhu: Wenluan Zhouqi* (Policy Hogs Replace Market Hogs: Disorderly Cycle)," Dahe Henan Provincial News Network, July 26, 2010. http://newpaper.dahe.cn/dhcf/page/402/2010-08-03/16/71641280791937281.pdf

Liu, Chunfang, and Jimin Wang. "Analysis of Recent Fluctuation in Our Country's Hog Prices and Future Trends" (in Chinese). Institute of Agricultural Economics, Chinese Academy of Agricultural Sciences, Research Briefing No. 218, May 20, 2009, and *Agricultural Outlook*, May 2009.

_____. "Status Quo and Prospect of Pig Industry Development in China" (in Chinese), *Agricultural Outlook*, Vol. 6, No. 3, March 2010, pp. 28-31.

Liu, Heguang, and Dongsheng Sun. "Development of China's Pig Meat Consumption and Its Prospect" (in Chinese), *Agricultural Outlook*, Vol. 6, No. 1, January 2010, pp. 35-38.

Liu, Yuman, Xiaoqing Yi, Yintong Du, and Lei Wang. "Issues of Food Quality and Safety in the Supply of Pork Chain," *Chinese Journal of Animal Science* 43(2), 2007.

Liu, Zhaozheng, "Study on Current Rural Environmental Problems," *Issues in Agricultural Economics*, 2009, Vol. 30, No. 3, pp. 70-73.

Nie, Fengying, Ling Dong, and Jieying Bi. "Fluctuation and Cycle of Pork Price in China." Selected paper presented at International Agricultural Economics Association meeting, Beijing, China, August 2009.

Petry, Mark, and Lei Zhang. *China's Corporate Income Tax Exemption for Agricultural Enterprises*. GAIN 9003. U.S. Department of Agriculture, Foreign Agricultural Service. January 13, 2009.

Ren, Xiaoming. "16 Questions on Treatment of Swine Fever (Zhu Gao Re Bing Shiliu Wenti)" (in Chinese), *Today's Animal Husbandry and Veterinary Medicine* (Jinri Xumu Shouyi), June 12, 2010.

Sun, De, Haiyan Jia, and Guochen Duan. "2011 Nian Zhu Jia Tui Shou Da Diao Cha (2011 Hog Price Survey)." Breeding Hog Information Net, June 2011. http://www.chinaswine.org.cn/piaofu/dc201105/dcjg.htm

Sun, Luwei. "Sheng Zhude Ying Kui Ping Hengdian Shi Zenyang Huifude (How the Breakeven Point for Hogs Was Reached)," *Farmers Daily*, August 3, 2010. http://nc.people.com.cn/GB/12329988.html

Van Arsdall, Roy N., and Kenneth E. Nelson. *U.S. Hog Industry*. Agriculture Economics Report No. 511. U.S. Department of Agriculture, Economic Research Service, June 1984.

Wang, Yan'an. "*Yi Tou Zhude Jianyi zhi Lu* (A Pig's Quarantine Trip)," *Economic Observer News*, May 8, 2009.

Wang, Fanghao, Wenqi Ma, Zhengxia Dou, Lin Ma, Liu Xiaoli, Junxiang Xu, and Fusuo Zhang. "The Estimate of the Production Amount of Animal Manure and its Environmental Effect in China" (in Chinese), *China Environmental Science*, 2006, Vol. 26, No. 5, pp. 614-617.

Woolsey, M., J. Zhang, and K. Rasmussen. *China Livestock and Products Annual Report*. GAIN CH10055, U.S. Department of Agriculture, September 24, 2010.

Woolsey, M., and J. Zhang. *U.S. Pork Exports to China on the Rise*. GAIN CH11020, U.S. Department of Agriculture, May 9, 2011.

Xiao, Hongbo, and Jimin Wang. "China's Hog Production Situation in 2008 and Its Prospects" (in Chinese), *Agricultural Outlook*, June 2009, pp. 16-18.

Xinhua News Agency. "Fa Gai Wei: Zhongguo Bu Keneng Daliang Cong Waiguo Jinkou Zhu Rou (Development and Reform Commission: China Cannot Import Large Amounts of Pork from Foreign Countries)," online news report, September 4, 2007.

Yang, Wan. "Zhu Sheng Bing le, Bu Ru Zhijie Deng Si Na Baoxian? (Sick Pigs, Better to Wait For Them To Die to Collect Insurance?)," *Yangzhou Daily News,* July 1, 2010. www.yznews.com.cn/news/2010-07/01/content_3278925.htm

Zhang, Xuebiao, and Nie Fengying. "Retrospect and Prospect of the Chinese Pork Market" (in Chinese). *Agricultural Outlook*, March 2010, pp. 19-22.

Zhang, Yi. "Hog Farming: If Not the 'Roller Coaster' Which Car to Ride?" (in Chinese), *Peoples Daily*, June 27, 2010. http://nc.people.com.cn/GB/11980484.html

Zhang, Yue. "Xu Qin Yangzhi Ye Chengwe Nongye Wuran Yuan zhi Shou (Livestock and Poultry Industry Have Become the Leading Source of Agricultural Pollution)," Xinhua News Service, December 5, 2010. www.gov.cn/jrzg/2010-12/05/content_1759746.htm

Zhou, Wangjun. "Positive Research on Stabilizing the Hog Market" (in Chinese). National Development and Reform Commission, May 2010. www.sdpc.gov.cn/zjgx/t20100525_348867.htm

Zhu, Zhigang. "Zhu Zhigang Answers Questions on Response to Rising Pork Prices and Promotion of Healthy Hog Industry Development" (in Chinese). Ministry of Finance Net, June 22, 2007. www.gov.cn/gzdt/2007-06/22/content_657983.htm

www.ingramcontent.com/pod-product-compliance
Lightning Source LLC
Chambersburg PA
CBHW041305180526
45172CB00003B/974